FAIRY DUSTERS

and

BLAZING STARS

EXPLORING WILDFLOWERS WITH CHILDREN

by Suzanne M. Samson

illustrated by Preston Neel

ROBERTS RINEHART PUBLISHERS

PUBLISHED IN THE UNITED STATES OF AMERICA
BY ROBERTS RINEHART PUBLISHERS
121 SECOND AVENUE, NIWOT, COLORADO 80544

ISBN 1-879373-81-5
LIBRARY OF CONGRESS CATALOG CARD NUMBER 94-65089

PRINTED AND BOUND IN HONG KONG BY COLORCORP/SING CHEONG

DISTRIBUTED IN THE U.S. AND CANADA BY PUBLISHERS GROUP WEST

For Dave

and in memory of Maximum Stryder

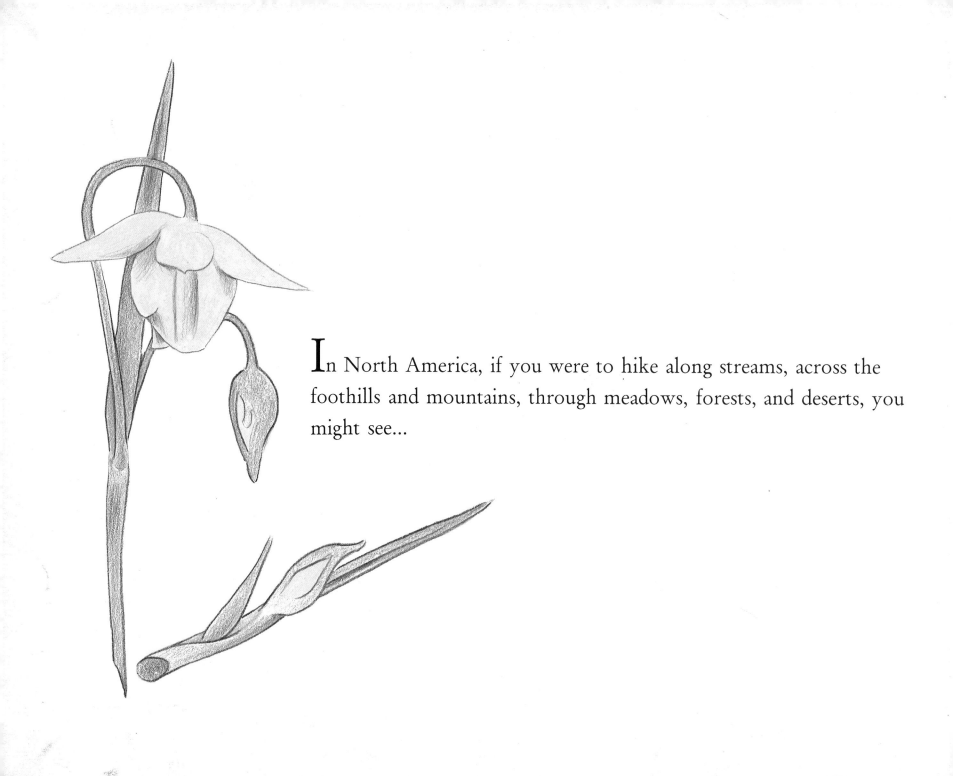

In North America, if you were to hike along streams, across the foothills and mountains, through meadows, forests, and deserts, you might see...

Fairy Lanterns
lighting your way,
or...

grinning Monkeyflowers out to play, or...

bright red Skyrockets blasting off, or...

Sneezeweed beginning to sneeze and cough, or...

firebreathing Snapdragons
having fun, or...

Labrador Tea being sipped in the sun, or...

Mule's Ears drooping in the heat, or...

Candysticks licked for
a special treat, or...

Mexican Hats providing shade, or...

Angel Trumpets leading a parade, or...

Pussy Paws pointing
everywhere, or...

Popcorn exploding into the air, or...

Ghost Flowers vanishing from sight, or...

Blazing Stars shining ever so bright, or...

Elephant Heads peeking at you, or..

Lady's Slippers being stepped into, or...

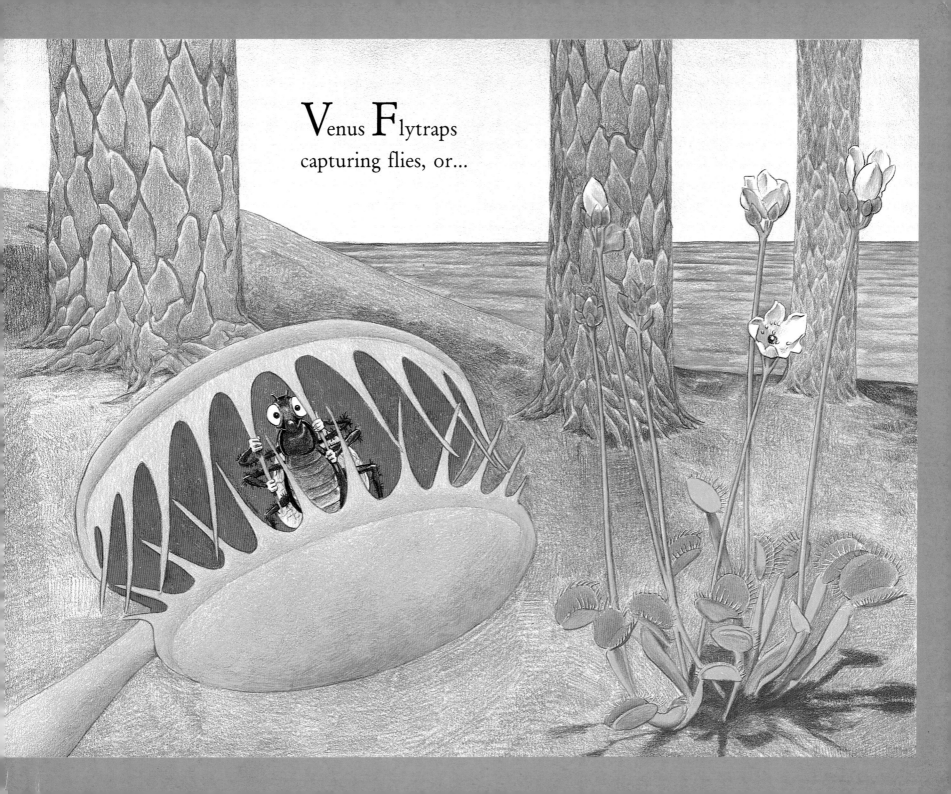

Venus Flytraps
capturing flies, or...

Turtlebacks wearing a cute disguise, or...

Paintbrushes painting
here and there, or...

Fairy **D**usters
dusting
everywhere, or...

Lizards' Tails bent towards the ground, or...

Baby Blue Eyes spying all around, or...

Steers' Heads staring off into space, or...

Firecrackers bursting all over the place, or...

an Indian Blanket on the ground, or...

Fairy Bells producing a pleasant sound, or..

an Indian Pipe being smoked alone, or...

a Jack-in-the-Pulpit observing his home, or...

Chinese Houses in wind and showers, or...

Shooting Stars
celebrating your discovery of wildflowers.

Golden Fairy Lantern
(aka Yellow Globe Lily)
Calochortus amabilis
April-June; Dry slopes
in shady thickets.
Northern California.

Lewis' Monkeyflower
Mimulus lewisii
June-August; wet areas in
mountains. Western Canada
to the Sierra Nevada in
California; higher mountains
of the Pacific states.

Skyrocket (aka Scarlet Gilia;
Desert Trumpet; Skunk Flower)
Ipomopsis aggregata
May-September; dry, rocky
slopes, often in open forests
or sagebrush. From Texas to
California, northward to
British Columbia.

Sneezeweed
Helenium autumnale
August-November; damp
thickets and meadows;
shores. Florida westward
to Texas and north to
Nebraska, Minnesota, and
Quebec.

Net-cup Snapdragon Vine
Maurandya wislizenii
April-July; along dunes and
among brush and shrubs.
Arizona and Texas southward
to Mexico.

Labrador Tea
Ledum groenlandicum
June-August; cold, swampy
ground, mountain summits.
Across Canada and Alaska,
and as far south as New
Jersey, Ohio, and Oregon.

Mule's Ears
Wyethia amplexicaulis
May-July; open hillsides, meadows and woods. Washington to Montana, south to Colorado, Utah, and Nevada.

Candystick (aka Sugarstick)
Allotropa virgata
May-August; shady, coniferous forests. British Columbia to central California.

Mexican Hat (aka Cone Flower)
Ratibida columnaris
July-October; open prairies. Great Plains; eastern Rocky Mountains; westward to Arizona, south into Mexico.

Angel Trumpets
Acleisanthes longiflora
May-September; sandy soil or rocky grades in deserts or on plains. Texas and New Mexico to southeastern California and Mexico.

Pussy Paws
Calyptridium umbellatum
May-August; coniferous forests, open mountain flats in sandy or gravelly soil. Baja California to British Columbia, eastward to Montana, Utah, and Wyoming.

Popcorn Flower
Plagiobothrys nothofulvus
March-May; open grassy places. Southern Washington to northern Baja.

Ghost Flower (aka Mojave Flower)
Mohavea confertiflora
March-April; sandy places and rocky slopes. Southern Nevada and western Arizona to the California deserts and into Baja.

Blazing Star
Mentzelia laevicaulis
June-October; dry, sandy regions. California to Washington; east to Montana and Utah.

Elephant Head
Pedicularis groenlandica
June-August; wet mountain meadows and along streambanks. Throughout the western mountains.

Pink Lady's Slipper
(aka Moccasin Flower)
Cypripedium acaule
April-July; forests, especially pinelands. Newfoundland to South Carolina and Georgia; west to Alabama, Tennessee and Minnesota.

Venus Flytrap
Dionaea muscipula
May-June; damp, sandy locations; among pines. North and South Carolina coastal plains.

Desert Turtleback
Psathyrotes ramosissima
March-June; dry, sandy soil. Mojave and Colorado Deserts into Mexico; northwest into Arizona and Utah.

Indian Paintbrush (aka
Painted Cup)
Castilleja coccinea
May-July; moist, sandy soil
in grassy meadows and
prairies. New England and
Manitoba to Florida; westward to Louisiana, Texas,
and Oklahoma.

Fairy Duster (aka Mesquitella)
Calliandra eriophylla
February-May; sandy or gravelly
slopes in deserts and arid
grasslands. Southern California to Texas and New Mexico;
south into Mexico.

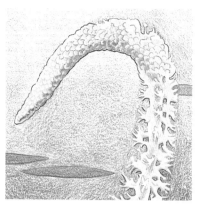

Lizard's Tail
(aka Water Dragon)
Saururus cernuus
June-September; swamps.
New England to Minnesota;
south to Florida; west to
Kansas, Missouri, and Texas.

Baby Blue Eyes
Nemophila menziesii
March-June; grassy hillsides
and moist fields. Central
Oregon, California.

Steer's Head
Dicentra uniflora
February-June; common
among sagebrush or gravelly
forest floors at high eleva-
tions. Northern California to
Washington; east to Utah and
Wyoming.

Firecracker Flower
Dichelostemma ida-maia
May-July; grassy slopes in
forest openings. Southwestern
Oregon to northwestern Cali-
fornia.

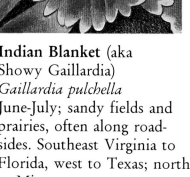

Indian Blanket (aka Showy Gaillardia)
Gaillardia pulchella
June-July; sandy fields and prairies, often along road-sides. Southeast Virginia to Florida, west to Texas; north to Minnesota.

Wartberry Fairybell
Disporum trachycarpum
May-July; wooded areas, streambanks. North coast ranges of California; Oregon to British Columbia; Rocky Mountain region; east to North Dakota.

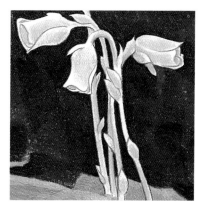

Indian Pipe
Monotropa uniflora
June-September; moist, shaded woods. Throughout the east; northwestern California to British Columbia.

Jack-in-the-pulpit
(aka Indian Turnip)
Arisaema triphyllum
April-June; damp woods and bogs. New Brunswick and Quebec south to Florida; west to Louisiana and Texas.

Purple Chinese Houses
(aka Innocence)
Collinsia heterophylla
March-June; shady places in sandy soil. California into northern Baja.

Shooting Star (aka Few Flowered or Western Shooting Star)
Dodecatheon pulchellum
April-August; coastal prairies, mountain meadows, riversides. Throughout the Western region.

REFERENCES

The Audubon Society Pocket Guides: Familiar Flowers of North America (Western Region) by Richard Spellenberg

The Audubon Society Field Guide to North American Wildflowers (Eastern Region) by William A. Niering and Nancy C. Olmstead

The Audubon Society Field Guide to North American Wildflowers (Western Region) by Richard Spellenberg

Wildflowers of North Carolina by William S. Justice and C. Ritchie Bell

Wildflowers of Yosemite by Lynn and Jim Wilson and Jeff Nicholas

California Desert Wildflowers by Philip A. Munz

The Odyssey Book of American Wildflowers by H.W. Rickett and Farrell Grehan

Wildflowers Across America by Lady Bird Johnson and Carlton B. Lees

Colorful Desert Wildflowers by Grace B. Ward and Onas M. Ward

Wildflowers of Western America by Robert T. Orr and Margaret C. Orr

Pacific States Wildflowers (Peterson Field Guides) by Theodore F. Niehaus and Charles L. Ripper

Wildflowers of the American West by Rose Houk

Sierra Wildflowers by Theodore F. Niehaus

A Sierra Nevada Flora by Norman F. Weeden

Wildflowers of the United States by H.W. Rickett (9 vols.)

The Macmillan Wild Flower Book by Clarence J. Hylander

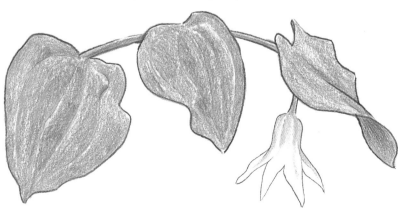